TIME VALUE OF MC

SNOWBALLING YOUR WAY TO FINANCIAL FREEDOM

JEREMY KHO

Copyright © 2017 by Jeremy Kho. All Right Reserved.

No part of this publication may be reproduced, distributed, or transmitted in any form or by any means, including photocopying, recording, or other electronic or mechanical methods, or by any information storage and retrieval system without the prior written permission of the publisher, except in the case of very brief quotations embodied in critical reviews and certain other noncommercial uses permitted by copyright law.

StressProofYourMoney.com

TABLE OF CONTENTS

Why I Wrote This Book	1
Why You Should Read This Book	3
Disclaimer	5
Preface	7
Relativity of Time and Money	13
Why Interest is so Interesting?	18
Beauty of Compounding Effect	23
Foundation for all Time Value of Money Problems	31
TVM in Mathematical Interpretation	39
Stay Ahead Of The Game	51
It's about Multiple Streams of Passive Income	55
What Does Financial Freedom Mean to You?	59
Bonus Material	63
About The Author	67
Other books by Jeremy Kho	69
One Last Thing...	71

Why I Wrote This Book

During my early 20s, like most millennials, I focused more on partying, buying expensive clothes, shoes, accessories and doing anything that contributed to fun, rather than learning how to manage my financesproperly. I wasted my early years and missed the opportunity to lay a foundation for investing wisely.

Only when I started my career did I become interested in money matters.During that period, I met my mentors who guided me and led me to the correct course on the importance of having a correct money mindset, they taught me that one must grasp the "language of money" and knowledge and exhibit discipline and persistence in applying the knowledge learned, only then can a rich life be possible.

Since then, I applied the concept and along the journey learned to make investing decisions with money. With the advice and techniques I learned from these great minds, books and courses, I earned a decent return on my finances and investment and moved a step closer to my life purpose!

I wrote this book because I wanted to make a difference in YOUR life the way my mentors inspired me. I wish to share the money techniques, tools and investing methods I've learned and used over the years in this book and I hope you will find the methods you wish you learned a long time ago. My goal is that you implement one or many techniques here so you can make the most of your money and investments, change your lifestyle and meet your goals and dreams!

Why You Should Read This Book

TVM is a very dull subject to start with. However, this is a language you and I must learn and understand. You wouldn't be able to make better financial decisions without IT, for you will just follow Blindly on whatever advice you get.

Your money depreciated because you trust that fair lady in the bank... your investment value evaporated because you support that financial adviser who was once your schoolmate...

This book is separated into 2 sections

1 The essential knowledge about TVM

2. The strategy you could apply that will improve your chance to financial freedom

Most financial books might bombard you with information and leave you to figure it all out yourself, they focus too much on tactics and fail to give advice on improving one's financial life. This book will focus on the very concept and advice regarding time value of money, some math behind it, and even provide you with spreadsheets where you can apply. This book will show you exactly what you need to learn about the time value of money. Most importantly, you will learn that working toward financial freedom is NOT IMPOSSIBLE when you understand the MATH behind TVM.

DISCLAIMER

These examples in the Book are provided as professional information for educational purposes only. The examples are a nonvalidated calculation for which there is absolutely no guarantee or warranty of fitness for a particular purpose or any purpose expressed or implied.

Any use of information contained herein assumes any and all responsibility and liability for use of the information including any misunderstanding, misuse or misapplication of the information.

Any use of these examples is "as is" and should only follow the user's independent confirmation that it produces valid results for the user before results are used for any purpose whatsoever.

In no event shall the author or stressproofyourmoney.com be liable for any incorrect or invalid results that are obtained by any use of the examples nor shall the author or stressproofyourmoney.com be liable for any loss of data, or profits or special incidental, indirect or consequential damages arising out of or in connection with the use of this Book.

PREFACE

Understanding the relationship between the value of money and time is fundamental when it comes to investing. Most of our financial decisions are strongly influenced by this relationship, and we must avoid confusion and misunderstandings. Next, we analyze the concept of the time value of money, understanding the ideas underlying the calculations to clarify concepts.

Why is the value of money influenced by the passage of time?

The concept of time value of money implies that a dollar received today has more value than a euro received in the future. This notion is easy to understand with a simple example: If you are given a choice between $500,000 today or $500,000 in 100 years, what do you prefer? Clearly, we see that the first option is better for the following reasons:

- Risk – The future is always uncertain. The money in hand is now 100% safe.
- Purchasing power – Due to inflation, you can buy many more things today with $500,000 that you can buy with those $500,000 in 100 years. If you look at it in reverse, you will see that $500,000 allowed you to buy many more things in 1916

than now. $500,000 in 1916 is equivalent to more than 10 million dollars today.
- Opportunity cost – A dollar received now can be invested, generating interest. On the other hand, a dollar received in the future cannot be invested until that future arrives. This inability to generate interest is called opportunity cost.

With these two clear ideas, we will see the two basic techniques used in any financial calculation involving a time horizon: compound interest also called annual compound growth, and process to calculate the present value.

The compound interest and the calculation of the present value: the basic tools to solve problems that involve amounts of money and a time horizon

Any problem that involves the calculation of the value of money in a temporary fragment is solved with two basic techniques: the compound interest and the calculation of the present value. These techniques allow us to compare today's dollars with dollars that we will receive at some future time.

Compound interest involves thinking about the value of money in the future. It consists of determining the future value of an investment made in the present, taking into account a series of possible periodic contributions.

Calculating the present value implies thinking about the value of money back in time. It consists of determining the present value of a quantity of money that will be received in the future, taking into account a series of possible periodic contributions. The present value is determined by applying a discount rate (opportunity cost) to the money that will be received in the future.

The 5 elements of any calculation of the time value of money

Now that we have seen the basic intuitions of compound interest and the calculation of present value, we are going to see the 5 elements that appear in any calculation that implies money and time. The 5 elements are: Periods, interest, Present Value, Payments, Future Value.

In short, understanding the time value of money is essential to achieving financial success, as this concept allows you to evaluate the potential value of money today in comparison to the future. When you talk about mortgages, loans, car notes and retirement funds, the practical knowledge of time value of money can help you accomplish the wealth you have longed for.

Jeremy

Stress Proof Your Money

The Essential of Time Value of Money

Relativity of Time and Money

Albert Einstein once quotes "Compound Interest is the 8th wonder of the world. He who understands IT, earns IT…He who doesn't…Pays IT."

Quite interesting, isn't it? But the fact is many barely knew IT, as IT can be seen in your savings, your daily expenditure via credit card, your loans, or mortgages. You might have already fallen victim to IT and paid the EXTRA without knowing IT!

Money, interest and time are all inter-related as they are relatives to each other, if you understand and use it properly, this wonder of compound interest will transform your hard-earned money into a state-of-the-art, highly powerful income-generating tool. Thus, in this session, we will explore what exactly is Time Value Money, compounding effect, and last but not least the mathematical formulation of TVM.

Understanding Time Value of Money

Time value of money, or in common abbreviation simply TVM, is the very foundation that the entire field of finance and commercial real estate is building upon. When we are dealing with savings, loans, mortgages, investment, and many other financial decisions, all can relate to TVM.

First you might ask, "Why does money have time value?"

One simple question, would you choose to receive 1000 dollars today or 1000 dollars in 12 months' time? Which option would you rather take? Let's look at an example below:

Mr. A, Mr. B, and Mr. C started working at 25 years old, and each of them saved 1000dollars every month until their retirement at 65.

Mr. C being an old-minded and conservative person had saved all the money in a safe deposit locker, and in 40 years, he had saved an amount of 480k.

Mr. B, who lived a balanced lifestyle, saved his money in a bank savings account with an annual rate of 1%, 40 years later, the savings amount become 592k.

As for Mr. A, who is very positive in the stock market, undertook an aggressive investment strategy and had gained himself an annual average return of 8% from the market. How much do you think he had earned? He had more than 3million after 40 years!

Have you noticed? Although all three of them started at the same age and saved an equal amount of money within the said period.

In your opinion, do you think that Mr. Conservative had made a good financial decision? Do you think that the dollar saved in his safe had the same value as today?

Understanding that time value of money is the economic principal that a dollar received today has greater value than a dollar received in the future, a dollar that you have today is worth more than a dollar you will receive in the future because you can invest it and earn interest. Thus, clearly one would choose to be A or B, and you will choose to receive the 1000 dollars now.

From this example, you can observe that there are 5 components of TVM, they are:

- **Periods** are evenly-spaced intervals of time. They are intentionally not stated in years since each interval must correspond to a compounding period for a single amount or a payment period for an annuity.

- **Payments** are a series of equal, evenly-spaced cash flows. In TVM applications, payments must represent all outflows (negative amount) or all inflows (positive amount).

- **Interest** is a charge for borrowing money, usually stated as a percentage of the amount borrowed over a specific period of time. **Simple interest** is computed only on the original amount borrowed. It is the return on that principal for one time period. In contrast, **compound interest** is calculated each period on the original amount borrowed **plus** all unpaid interest accumulated to date.

- **Present Value** is an amount today that is equivalent to a future payment, or series of payments, that has been discounted by an appropriate interest rate. The future amount can be a single sum that will be received at the end of the last period, as a series of equally-spaced payments (an annuity), or both. Since money has time value, the present value of a promised future amount is worth less the longer you have to wait to receive it.

- **Future Value** is the amount of money that an investment with a fixed, compounded interest rate will grow to by some future date. The investment can be a single sum deposited at the beginning of the first period, a series of equally-spaced payments (an annuity), or both. Since money has time value, we naturally expect the future value to be greater than the present value. The difference between the two depends on the number of compounding periods involved and the going interest rate.

WHY INTEREST IS SO INTERESTING?

Simply put, it is how much money paid for the money borrowed (which can expressed as a percentage or an amount), subjected to your credit history, you may have noticed different places charge different percentage at different times, but these are often based on a country prime rate which is determined by a country's central banking.

So, when you go to a bank for a loan of 10k and the local bank says 5% interest, in such condition, you are the *Borrower*, the Bank is the *Lender*, the *Principal* of the Loan will be 10k and the *Interest* as 5%.

Here the Bank charges you either Simple Interest or Compound Interest, take a look at the diagram below:

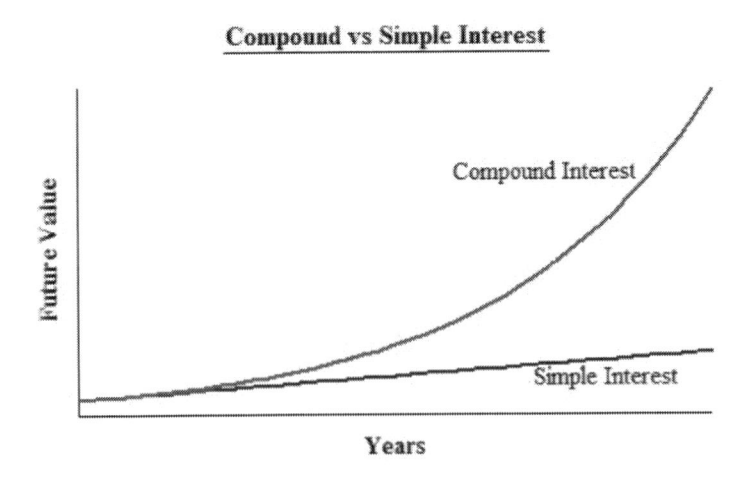

Figure 1: Compound vs simple interest

(https://tinyurl.com/kdwftoa)

The compound interest would grow in the exponential function as compared to linear function of simple interest as the time of the loan elapses. What you paid for simple interest is what you pay the same amount of every year, but with compound interest, the interest for the first period was added to the total, and the interest was calculated for the next period and so on. It is like paying interest on interest every period and this does not necessarily have to be paid per year, it could be per month or per day.

Thus, the same rules apply:

If it is simple interest, just work out the interest for one period, and multiply by the number of periods.

If it is compound interest, work out the interest for the first period, add it on and then calculate the interest for the next period.

Sometimes, you must have wondered, why the bank personnel was such a good guy and offered you a low interest rate for a 30-year loan. Well, they are not! As most banks work on compound interest, and compounded not on per year but on per month basis.

Does that mean that compound interest is a bad thing? Hell no, you can make them work for you! Instead of being a borrower, you can become the lender yourself and put your money in investment products, such as in a bank or a business so your money could grow. If you invest your money at a good interest rate, and over long periods it can grow very nicely!

UNDERSTAND THE RULE OF 72

"For any amount, which is compounding periodically at a fixed growth rate, the number of periods required for that amount to double can be estimated by dividing the percentage growth rate into 72."

It is a quick and easy way for investors to work out how many years it would take an investment to, theoretically, double in value. It also works if you need to estimate how long it would take for a sum of money to halve in value too.

Let's say an investment is expected to return 10% a year. So, 72/10 = 7.2. It would thus take roughly seven years for the investment to double. Now let's assume that the rate of inflation is 5% with 72/5 = 14.1, fourteen years from now, your savings would have lost half of its purchasing power.

However, it provides a good approximation for annual compounding, and for compounding at lower rates of returns only, generally from 4% to 15%. The approximations are less accurate at higher interest rates.

Comparison of rule of 72 and exact calculation as below:

Rate (%)	Rule of 72	Actual Periods
1	72	69.661
5	14.4	14.207
10	7.2	7.273
25	2.88	3.106
50	1.44	1.71
100	0.72	1

BEAUTY OF **C**OMPOUNDING **E**FFECT

The Compound Effect is the principle of reaping huge rewards from a series of small, smart choices. This small, smart choice can be on improving your health, relationships, finances or anything else for that matter in your life. The choices in the moment won't feel significant and you wouldn't notice any changes, you will not see immediate result.

If so, why do we bother? Most people get owned by the simplicity of the effect. For instance, they quit after a few weeks of running because they're still overweight. Or, they stop making contributions to their retirement account after a few years because they could use the cash now as it doesn't seem to be adding up. What they don't realize is that these small, seemingly insignificant steps completed consistently over time will create a radical difference.

An expert in his field does not become a pro in days, he has to dedicate most of his time to practicing almost every single day. And we know it takes a longer term in a healthy way to lose weight! Compounding effect is that simple, consistence and persistence are the keys, knowing practice does make perfection!

Then what does it have to do with your money? There's no real secret behind Buffett's wealth, simply Warren Buffett understands the power of compounding. Also, explains why Mr. A in our example earlier had the most net worth. Wealthy people know about compound interest and had worked to reinvest their investment's earnings, and over time had their net worth sky-rocketed!

Thus, the compounding effect in investment is the process of generating earnings on an asset's reinvested earnings. Two things it requires to work, the re-investment of earnings and time. The more time you give your investments, the more you are able to accelerate the income potential of your original investment, thus taking the pressure off of you.

PRESENT VALUE (PV) AND FUTURE VALUE (FV)

We know that a future value (FV) equals a present value (PV) plus the interest that can be earned by having ownership of the money; it is the amount that the PV will grow to over some stated period of time. Conversely, a present value equals the future value minus the interest that comes from ownership of the money; it is today's value of a future amount to be received at some specified time in the future.

The FV is calculated by multiplying the present value by the accumulation function and this value does not include inflation or other factors that affect the true value of money in the future. The process of finding the FV is often called Compounding and on the other hand, PV is the value on a given date of a payment or series of payments made at other times. The process of finding the PV from the FV is called Discounting.

PV and FV are inter-related; in which they are subjected by remaining variables or components of TMV, which are periods, payments and interest. So, when if the interest rate and number of periods remain constant, FV will increase as PV increases.

However, when the variable of the payment is fixed, the higher the interest rates go, the lower the PV and the higher the FV, this means that when another variable are considered that is the number of periods. The more time that passes, more interest will be accumulated per period, therefore the higher the FV will be if the PV is constant, and vice versa.

When dealing with PV and FV, often we are dealing with payments, and it can be a single payment or multiple payments, in which the next topic we will explore another term of TVM, that is Annuities.

WHAT IS ANNUITY?

Now that we have covered both PV and FV, we need to know about Annuity. In finance, an annuity is any series of equal payments(either paid by you or to be paid to you) that are made at regular intervals. The interval periods between payments are most commonly in years, half-yearly, months or weeks, so long the interval is consistent, an annuity can last for a short duration, say a few months or a long duration for decades.

Annuity simply is an agreement (i.e. bank or insurance company) in which you make one or multiple payments in exchange for receiving a set amount of income for a period of time. There are two basic types of annuities: ordinary annuities and annuities due.

- **Ordinary Annuity**: The payment comes at the end of the covered term. The common examples are the home mortgage, payments on installment loans or the interest payments from bonds. Take mortgage payments for instance, when you pay your mortgage on Feb. 1, you are paying for the use of your home for January, and you will pay for February in the following month and so on.

- **Annuity Due**: The payment comes at the beginning of the term, rent is an example of annuity due, and so when you pay the apartment rent on Jan. 1, you are paying for the use of the apartment in January, in which your first rent payment is due when you move in. Another common example of an annuity due is an insurance premium, where you pay today for future coverage.

In general, if you're the one that's making payments, an ordinary annuity is preferred, whereas if payments are paid to you, you are better off with an annuity due. Due to the TVM of money, a sum of money today will be worth much more compared to the equal amount in the future, therefore the longer you can delay making your first fixed payment, the less that payment costs you. On the other hand, the earlier you can receive the first payment of an annuity, the more it will be worth.

Apart from ordinary annuity and annuity due, there are other types of annuity, they are:

- *Fixed Annuity*: in which it pays out a fixed rate of return on your money, meaning that the income stream is guaranteed regardless of what's going on in the financial markets.

- *Variable Annuity*: Where variable rate of returns on your money were paid, this usually has a minimum guaranteed amount but can increase subject to the underlying investments such as stocks or funds.

- *Indexed Annuity*: it pays out a rate of return on your money based on an economic index, such as the S&P 500, or STI. It is a combination of the fixed and variables types as there's minimum guaranteed and it also enables you to enjoy a higher return when there are gains in the market

Therefore, annuitized payouts are important because they're the key to retirement accounts. You start with a lump sum at the start of retirement, and assuming it's invested at a set rate of return, you start to draw money out annually, we will explore how annuity affects the PV and FV of any amount of money in latter sessions.

FOUNDATION FOR ALL TIME VALUE OF MONEY PROBLEMS

All time value of money problems involves two fundamental techniques: compounding and discounting. Compounding and discounting is a process used to compare dollars in our pocket today versus dollars we have to wait to receive at some time in the future. Before we dive into specific time value of money examples, let's first review these basic building blocks.

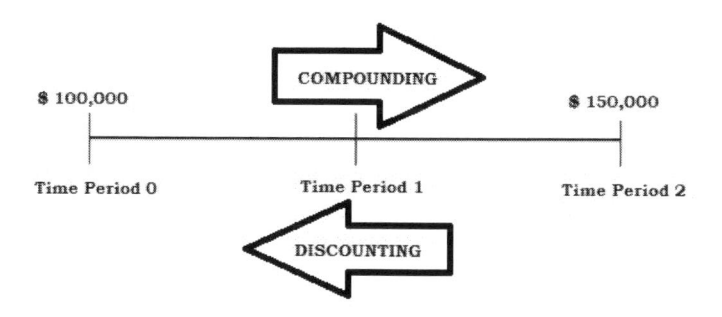

Figure 2: Compounding and Discounting

- **Compounding** is about moving money forward in time. It's the process of determining the future value of an investment made today and/or the future value of a series of equal payments made over time (periodic payments).

- **Discounting** is about moving money backwards in time. It's the process of determining the present value of money to be received in the future (as a lump sum and/or as periodic payments). Present value is determined by applying a discount rate (opportunity cost) to the sums of money to be received in the future.

So, when solving for the future value of money we set aside today, we compound our investment at a particular rate of interest. When solving for the present value of future cash flows, the problem is one of **discounting** rather than **growing** and the required expected return acts as the **discount rate.** In other words, discounting is merely the inverse of growing.

Understanding Cash Flow Diagram

Now that we understand the components of TVM, when dealing with some financial problems, it is best to be describe cash flow via some series of diagrams which will help to visualize the problem and show all inflows and outflows of cash along a timeline.

Hence a cash flow diagram allows you to graphically illustrate the timing of the cash (be it inflows of cash or outflows of cash). A cash flow diagram has a horizontal timeline subdivided into equal periods such as days, months or years. For each cash flow some payment or receipt will be plotted along this line at which it occurs whether at the beginning or at end of the period. There can be positive cash flow where each is represented by arrows which extend upward or downward from the time line with their bases at the appropriate positions along the timeline.

It is important to understand that funds that you receive such as proceeds from a mortgage or withdrawals from a savings account are positive cash flows represented by arrows extending upward from the time line with their bases at the appropriate positions along the timeline. While funds that you pay out such as savings deposits or lease payments are negative cash flows that are represented by arrows which extend downward from the line. One helpful way to think about a negative sign simply is money is flowing out of your pocket, a positive sign means money is flowing into your pocket.

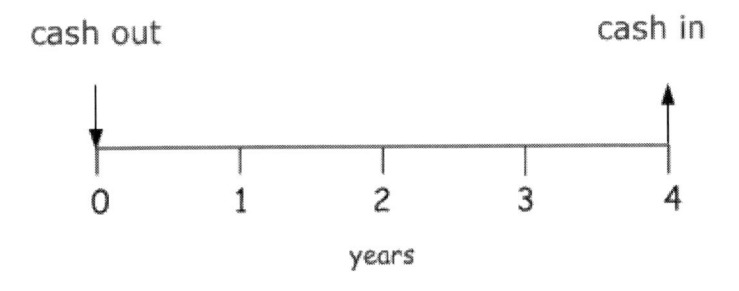

Figure 3: Cash Flow Diagram

https://tinyurl.com/kw2wyny

In short if you have X (PV) amount in your savings account, that amount of money that you have now is a negative cash outflow where you will treat it as though you were just now depositing it into the account. It might seem confusing with the pointing or arrows, but if you understand what they represent, really it doesn't matter how you draw your arrows.

We know that there are always two sides to a financial problem: a borrower and a lender; a buyer and a seller; an investor and an investment. You should keep in mind the dual nature of financial problems when drawing a cash flow diagram. From whose perspective will it be drawn? The example of a simple loan will be shown below. From the borrower's perspective, the transaction consists of a large cash inflow followed by a series of smaller cash outflows while that situation is exactly reversed for the lender:

Borrower's Perspective

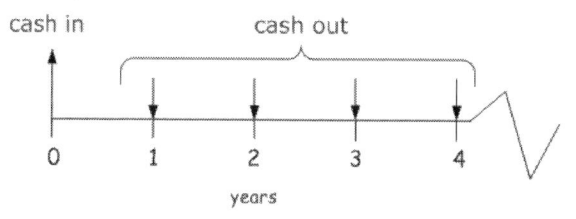

Lender's Perspective

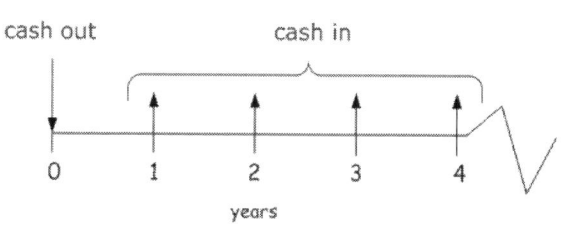

Figure 4: Borrower vs Lender

https://tinyurl.com/k9k4zkk

Note that the amounts calculated (PV or FV, payment amount, interest rate, number of periods) will be the same regardless of the perspective from which the cash flow diagram is drawn. It simply helps in understanding and describing the problem and to be conscious of the perspective from which it is viewed. Hence cash flow diagram's purpose is depicting a complex financial problems concisely and precisely as possible.

6 Basic Types of Cash Flow Diagram

Present Value (PV) of a Single Sum

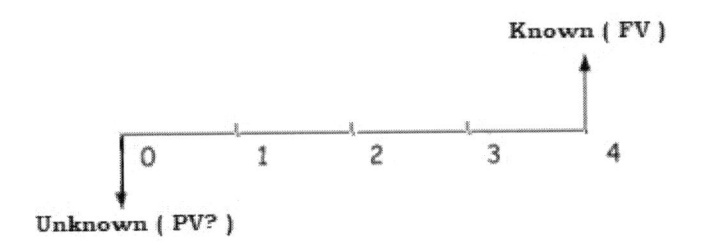

```
                              Known ( FV )
                                   ↑
       ┌────┬────┬────┬────┐
       │ 0    1    2    3    4
       ↓
    Unknown ( PV? )
```

Future Value (FV) of a Single Sum

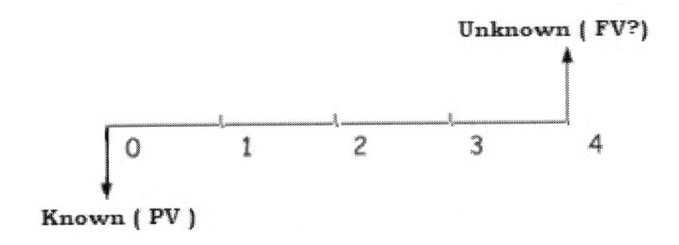

```
                              Unknown ( FV? )
                                   ↑
       ┌────┬────┬────┬────┐
       │ 0    1    2    3    4
       ↓
    Known ( PV )
```

Present Value (PV) of an Ordinary Annuity

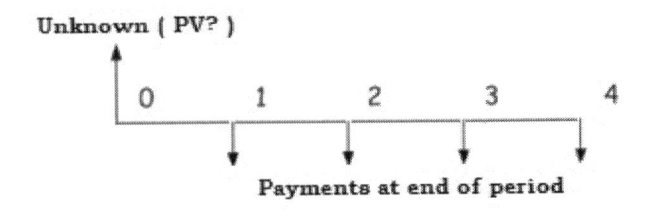

```
   Unknown ( PV? )
        ↑
        │  0    1    2    3    4
        └──────┬────┬────┬────┤
                ↓    ↓    ↓    ↓
              Payments at end of period
```

36

Future Value (FV) of an Ordinary Annuity

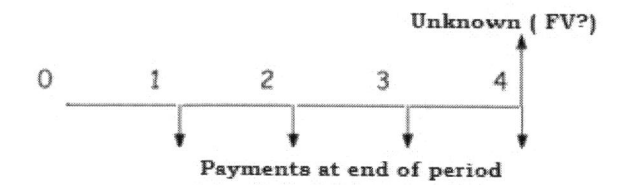

```
                              Unknown ( FV?)
                                    ▲
   0      1      2      3      4
          │      │      │      │
          ▼      ▼      ▼      ▼
          Payments at end of period
```

Present Value (PV) of an Annuity Due

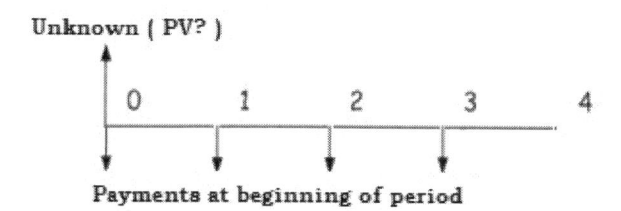

```
Unknown ( PV? )
    ▲
    │   0      1      2      3      4
    ▼   ▼      ▼      ▼      ▼
       Payments at beginning of period
```

Future Value (FV) of an Annuity Due

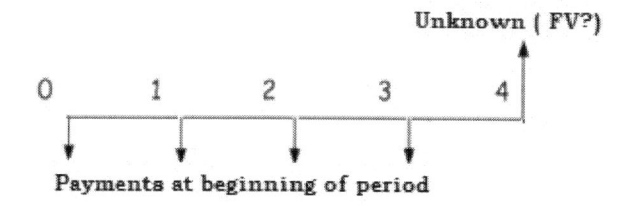

```
                              Unknown ( FV?)
                                    ▲
   0      1      2      3      4
   │      │      │      │
   ▼      ▼      ▼      ▼
   Payments at beginning of period
```

TVM in Mathematical Interpretation

Once we grasp the meaning of the 5 components of TVM, that is *PV*, *FV*, Payments (*PMT*), interest (*i*) and period (*n*), and with the help of cash flow diagram, solving any TVM problem would be easy with help of Excel function. In general, there are 6 basic types of TVM problems:

Present Value (PV) of a Single Sum

The TVM problem discounts a single future amount to a present value. A simple example would be: A bond will be worth $10,000 in 10 years. What should you pay for it today to earn 5% annually?

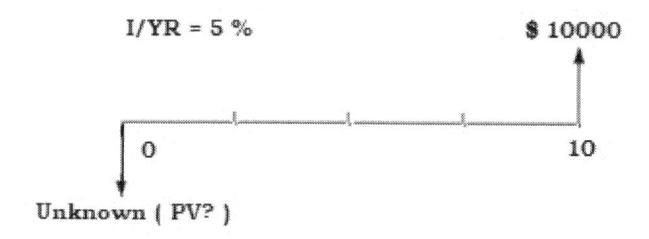

I/YR = 5 % $ 10000

0   10

Unknown (PV?)

There are 4 components in play. We are given the future value *FV* of $10,000, the number of periods *n* is 10 years, and the interest, *at* 5% per year. Unknown PV can be solved:

$$PV = \frac{FV}{(1+i)^n} = (\$\,6139.13)$$

Future Value (FV) of a Single Sum

The TVM problem compounds a single amount to a future value. Here's an example: What will $10,000 invested today for 5 years grow to be worth if compounded annually at 10% per year?

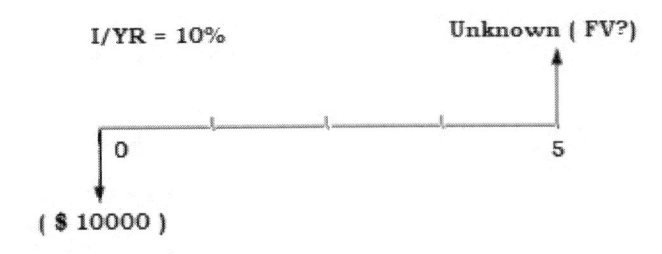

```
      I/YR = 10%                    Unknown ( FV?)
                                         ↑
      ┌─────┴─────┴─────┴─────┴─────┴
      │ 0                           5
      ↓
   ( $ 10000 )
```

Again, 4 known components were identified, we know the present value PV is ($10,000). It's negative because it's outflow of cash when we invested in an investment today. The number of period n is 5 years, and the interest i is 10%. We solved:

$FV = PV(1 + i)^n = \$ 16105.10$

Present Value (PV) of an Ordinary Annuity

The problem discounts an annuity (of series of equal payments) to a present value. An example of this type of time value of money problem: An insurance company is offering an annuity that pays $25,000 per year for the next 4 years. How much should you pay for the annuity to earn 5% per year?

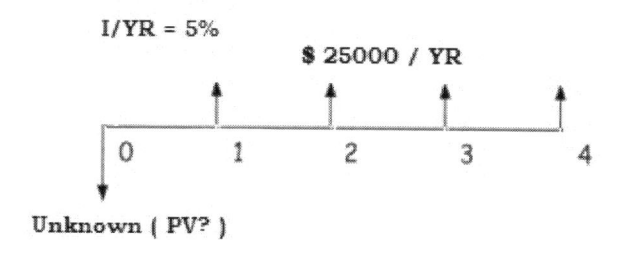

```
                I/YR = 5%
                                $ 25000 / YR
                    ↑       ↑       ↑       ↑
        ┌───────┼───────┼───────┼───────┤
        │   0       1       2       3       4
        ↓
    Unknown ( PV? )
```

Here we know that the payment *PMT* is $25,000 per year, with period *n* being 4 years and the interest rate *i* is 5% per year. By solving

$$PV_{OA} = PMT(\frac{1-(1+i)^{-n}}{i}) = (\$\,8864.88)$$

FUTURE VALUE (FV) OF AN ORDINARY ANNUITY

This TVM problem compounds an annuity to a future value. An example is as follows: If you deposit $10,000 at the end of each year for 4 years earning 5% annually, how much money will be in the account at the end of year 4?

```
I/YR = 5%                    Unknown ( FV?)

0        1        2        3        4

         ( $ 10000 ) / YR
```

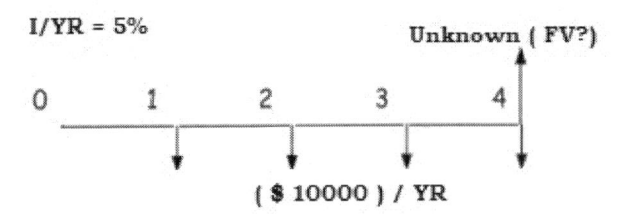

Four known components are identified. The payment amount *PMT* is -$10,000 as we are depositing at the end of each year. Interest rate is 5% and the total periods *n* is 4 years. As we aren't starting with anything, our present value is simply $0. We can easily solve for the future value

$$FV_{OA} = PMT\left(\frac{(1+i)^n - 1}{i}\right) = \$\,43101.25$$

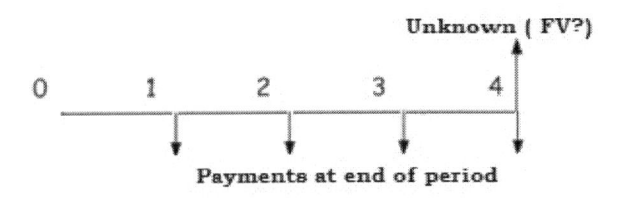

```
                             Unknown ( FV?)

0        1        2        3        4

         Payments at end of period
```

PRESENT VALUE (PV) OF AN ANNUITY DUE

This problem is common for calculating the present value of your future rent payments as specified in a lease you sign with your landlord in which we need to discount the formula one period forward as the payments are held for a lesser amount of time.

So, when calculating the present value, we assume that the first payment was made today. Let's take the same example of ordinary annuity earlier, it would give;

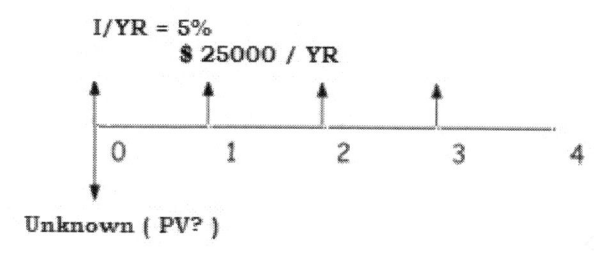

```
                I/YR = 5%
                $ 25000 / YR
        ┌────┬────┬────┬────┬────
        0    1    2    3    4
        │
   Unknown ( PV? )
```

Thus, given payment *PMT* is $25,000 at the start of each year, with period *n* being 4 years and the interest rate *i* is 5% per year. By solving

$$PV_{AD} = PMT\left(\frac{1 - (1+i)^{-n}}{i}\right)(1+i) = (\$\,9308.12)$$

Recall that the present value of an ordinary annuity returned a value of $8864.88. The present value of an ordinary annuity is less than that of an annuity due because the further back we discount a future payment, the lower its present value: each payment or cash flow in an ordinary annuity occurs one period further into the future.

Future Value (FV) of an Annuity Due

When you are receiving or paying cash flows for an annuity due, payment in the series is made one period sooner, thus each amount is held longer at the end of the period. Take the example given earlier example and we have;

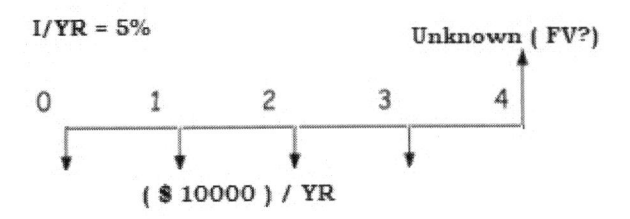

```
I/YR = 5%                              Unknown ( FV?)

0        1        2        3        4
         ( $ 10000 ) / YR
```

The payment amount *PMT* is -$10,000 but is depositing at the start of each year. Interest rate *i* is 5% and the total period *n* is 4 years. We can solve for the future value

$$FV_{AD} = PMT\left(\frac{(1+i)^n - 1}{i}\right)(1+i) = \$\,45256.31$$

Note the difference of FV of an annuity due to that of ordinary annuity? It ends up higher as the amount was held longer which in favor of your deposits.

Other Types of TVM Problems

- **Amount needed to amortize a present value**

This TVM problem determines a series of equal payments necessary to amortize a present value. An example: What are the yearly repayments on a 4-year loan of $10,000 at an annual rate of 5%?

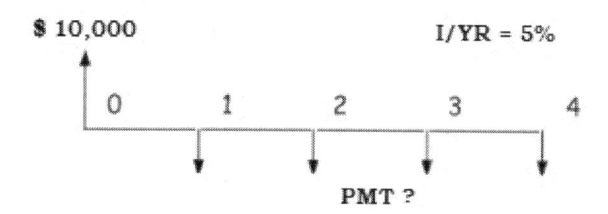

In this problem, we are given the total number of period n as 4 years, a present value PV of $10,000, an annual interest rate i of 5% and it is implied that the future value FV is $0. Thus, we can solve

$$PMT = PV\left(\frac{i}{1-(1+i)^{-n}}\right) = \$\,2820.12$$

- **Payments needed to achieve a future value**

This TVM problem compounds a series of equal payments into a future value. An example: At a 5% interest rate, how much needs to be deposited each year over the next 4 years to grow to be exactly $10,000?

```
            I/YR = 5%                    $ 10,000

        0       1       2       3       4
                ↓       ↓       ↓       ↓
                        PMT ?
```

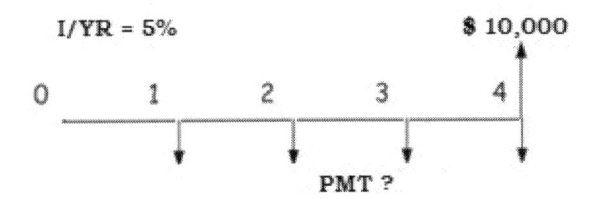

The 4 known variables are the rate *i* at 5%, the total number of periods *n* which is 4 years, and future value *FV* we are trying to achieve is $10,000. Assuming payments occur at the start of each year, the equation will be,

$$PMT = FV\left(\frac{i}{(1+i)^{n+1} - (1+i)}\right) = \$2209.64$$

However, if payment is to occur at the end of each year, that will give one less interest period where

$$PMT = FV\left(\frac{i}{(1+i)^n - 1}\right) = \$2320.12$$

Note how time factored to the TVM problems, whether payment was done before a period or at the end of a period matters. Although you might not notice a huge difference, but when the amount dealing is large, and over a long period, the compounding effect is significant!

Final Word

In solving TVM problems, it is important to note that both the number of periods and the rate of interest are to express consistency. Say the rate and the number of periods are both expressed in years, but if the payment frequency of a problem is expressed monthly, some conversion is required to avoid causing any conflict in the formula.

When we are dealing with loans, investment analysis, capital budgeting, and many other financial decisions, the TVM is impossible to ignore. Its concepts are the core of valuation of personal financial. Thus, to have a solid foundation for understanding time value of money will pay dividends for years to come. Understanding it is a guarantee for you to become rich in time to come.

ACHIEVING FINANCIAL FREEDOM IN THE YEARS AHEAD

<u>Stay Ahead Of The Game</u>

"Think What You Do When You Run in Debt: You Give to Another Power over Your Liberty" ~Benjamin Franklin

Debt is your number one priority, get rid of the bad debt! Stop paying more interests to the bank, stop getting into further debt! Focus on paying off your debt instead! Pay your debt on time! No more late payment, those are bad.

Here are some suggestions.

PRIORITIZE YOUR DEBT

When you have more than one debt to pay, it would be rational to pay off the debt with the highest rate of interest. Avoid paying interest on the interest you already owe because you didn't make enough payment to reduce the balance. Therefore, it is important for us to pay off high interest incurring debts first, else, we could be paying twice the original amount. Consider what you stand to lose for non-payment. Priority debts should also be those that have bad consequences if you don't pay. For example, you may lose your home if you default on your mortgage payments or get a bad credit score, legal action could be taken against you for credit card outstanding debts.

PAY OFF THE LOWEST DEBT BALANCE FIRST

This practice is known as the "snowball technique." It is like rolling down a snowy hill, forming a snowball. The snowball will grow larger and faster as it rolls further down. As the amount of money you send into each payment gradually compounds, each debt is reduced until you are sending in large amounts of cash to pay off your biggest and final debt. The snowball technique helps to repay your high-interest balances far faster than you could by just using a random payment arrangement.

MAKE MICROPAYMENTS TO REDUCE DEBT

These payments can start off with a small amount and over time add up to big balance reductions which save you thousands in interest expense. Every time you gather some funds, regardless of the amount, use it to pay off your outstanding debt payment. If you were to keep the amount, you would most probably spend it on something else, it is human nature. People often ignore the power of small amounts, your small efforts may not look like they're even denting your debt, but there is a compounding effect that is at work. Over the years, your debt will be eventually paid off.

Pay off debts regularly

The single most important thing you can do to pay off debts is to pay your bills on time, whether it is the full amount of just part of the amount. Paying your bills on time is absolutely critical, as missing one payment on your credit card may result in a late fee, late payments often trigger rate increases on your other credit cards. Thus, setting up an automatic repayment will ensure you don't miss your payment. Whenever you receive extra funds from an overtime work schedule or claim reimbursement, increase your debt repayment amount, by doing so, you can reduce your debt faster.

Snowballing Your Way to Wealth

Saving will be your next priority. The very first step of a good personal saving advice is: **Don't set any percentage from your earnings to saving just YET**. Depending on what or where you work, you might be earning a salary of 20k or a nice 6-figure salary, but if you are the former, asking you to save up to 50% of your earnings would sound impossible.

The first step is to decide how your earnings flow and answer the following questions.

- Where and how do you spend?
- Do you have any debt to pay?
- What sort of commitment do you have?

- Do you have any investment strategy or plan?

List everything out, access and budget your financial situation and cut those unnecessary expenses. Only then will you have an idea how much you could save.

The trick now is how do you save and not spend that extra money? Paying yourself first is the important step. Start by linking and set up an automatic transfer from your checking account to savings account, saving becomes much painless. It could be a fixed amount or percentage or whatever you think you can afford.

Remember you could start-up small if you just started your career, budget how your money flows and build it up when your income increase.

It's about Multiple Streams of Passive Income

Now that you have cleared your debt and you have some savings, does that mean you're a step closer to financial freedom? Yes and No.

Yes, in the sense that you will be steps ahead of the majority who are still paying the interests on their debts. No, because depending on a single source of income is a bad idea to plan your way to financial independence.

You're Doing It Wrong!

The one behavior that differentiates the rich and the mediocre is that the rich make use of the power of TVM, they leverage their money and create not one but multiple passive income streams.

This is some excerpt taken from MJ DeMarco's book *"The Millionaire Fastlane,"*

"How is money passive? If you have a lot of money, you're given the gate key to switch teams from consumer to producer. Specifically, you move from borrower to lender. You move from employee to employer. You move from customer to owner. In other words, people pay to use YOUR MONEY in the form of interest or ownership."

How?

Here are some steps to get you started on the journey, for any young and new investor, I'd like to focus on 3 points:

- **Start up small and reinvest the dividends.**

Don't get the misconception that you need to have a lot of money before you can invest, you could invest by a monthly contribution from as little as $100 in low-cost index fund, and taking advantage of the reinvestment, most brokerages nowadays offer a no-fee, no-commission reinvestment program.

- **Invest for the long term, always.**

Don't fear the unknown, age and time are the best assets you have. Because of the compounding effect, for example when you invest money in the index fund, your money can grow very nicely over long periods.

- **Diversification, don't put all your eggs in one basket.**

This is especially true for new investors, don't risk your capital in a single stock or bond even if you have gone through the analysis and are very sure what you have picked.

As the aim is to transform the money into a passive income stream, in a way it is about leveraging your money through the power of TVM. Therefore, the investment is not necessarily limited to Stocks or Equities, it could be your next big idea, business or even your own self!

What Does Financial Freedom Mean to You?

Do you still hold the concept that financial freedom is about becoming a multimillionaire? Then you've got it Wrong!

So, you need to figure out what financial freedom means to you:

- *What do you want?*
- *What is your purpose?*
- *What is it you want in life?*

If you are blindly chasing the numbers, say 1 million, then you would want 2, next 4... as when you do so, you don't own the money, the money owns you!

"Financial freedom has nothing to do with the money. It has to do with your freedom."

You need to have some goals or purposes attached. Only then you will be able to work out the number that will give you freedom and control over your life.

Now, where to find the next income stream?

Here are some lists where you can get started right away. And I am sure you will like them as it won't break your bank!

- **The Millennial Roadmap to a Rich Life (https://www.amazon.com/dp/B01LX2PMXD)**

– In this book, I shared my strategy and system on personal finance and investing, and you will surely learn how to create a second source of income through investments.

- **Amazon Affiliate Program (https://affiliate-program.amazon.com/)**

- The Associates Program permits you to monetize your website, social media user-generated content, or online software application…

- **Wealthy Affiliate (https://www.wealthyaffiliate.com?a_aid=5cba9f7c)**

–if you want to venture into the online business world, wealthy affiliate is a great starter. You can start off the basic training for free, and when you are ready to commit, you will see that WA had lots of potential compared to other similar products that cost thousands of dollar.

- **Fiverr (https://www.fiverr.com/s2/34fbc171e2)**

- Some of you might already know about this site. It is the world's largest marketplace for services, so if you have some skills, you can provide your service here, and work out the alternate source of income from your spare time. A great place to get work outsourced as well.

These are just a few that I recommended, there are other types of income source that you can consider, for instance, the crowdfunding platform, if you got a great idea, consider the use of Kickstarter, GoFundMe, and Indiegogo.

Next, you have Patreon, an internet-based platform that allows content creators to build their own subscription content service.

Last but not least, the e-commerce platform. To name a few, such as Etsy, shopify or ebay.

If you feel that you don't have a great idea, in creating own products/services. Here are 8 lists where you could learn to improve your skill or new ability.

- Coursera (https://www.coursera.org/)
- Lynda.com (https://www.lynda.com/)
- Codecademy (https://www.codecademy.com/)
- WA (https://www.wealthyaffiliate.com?a_aid=5cba9f7c)
- Udemy (https://www.udemy.com/)
- Skillshare (https://www.skillshare.com/)
- General Assembly (https://generalassemb.ly/)
- Stanford Online (http://online.stanford.edu/)

From coding to app development, writing to book publication. You can find from these site.

The truth is the opportunity to your next income stream is everywhere. The resources are readily available for you. However, do not expect fast results, you need times to build those. Do not feel discouraged when you don't see the result immediately. Remember the power of TVM, it takes momentum to built, but then every action you took today will come in multiple tomorrow.

Really, the secret to successfully creating the next income source lies in you. Do not underestimate yourself. I will end the book with quote by *Steve Maraboli*,

"Don't just dream of success, create a plan and act upon it! Your momentum creates the door upon which opportunity knocks"

BONUS MATERIAL

Now because I wanted this book to make sense to everybody. Nope, I don't want you saying "Oh, so that's TVM…" Nope, I want you to Apply it!

This is what you need to do next:

Visit https://stressproofyourmoney.com , and subscribe to the newsletter, and you will be receiving SPYM Financial Assistant.

"INTRODUCING THE SPYM FINANCIAL ASSISTANT"

SPYM Financial Assistant comes with 6 powerful features (Present Value, Future Value, Annuity Value, Compound Interest, Loan (by paid amount), Loan (by loan terms). The tool is not a simple TVM calculator as lots of efforts were put into while creating it, from researching to coding and testing, as well as result comparison with the actual data from banks. It is a tool to give you a leg-up to achieve something you couldn't have done alone, it aims to help you to:

Plan your saving goals

Using the compound interest calculator, you can compare saving rates from different banks, decide how much to put into saving in order to meet your goals, be it short, mid or long term. So, you will get to save more of your dollars.

Forecast your investment returns

Present and Future Value is a calculator that allows you to simulate your investment return, be it an asset or equity, you can decide if an amount is invested now or at a later stage, in order to reap a maximum profit so you can invest with confidence.

Retirement planning

The annuity value calculator can help you to decide how much of the funds to be invested in your retirement account. With this, you can also decide which life insurance is suitable to your needs so you can put your mind at ease.

Compare the loans, credit cards,

The Loan (by loan terms) calculator will help you to compare different credit card rates or loans and mortgages. You can take a peek at how much of loans and interest you are paying for different rates. So, you can save thousands of dollars from paying interests.

Organize your loans and credit cards repayment

The Loan (by paid amount) calculator will save your precious time as you organize your budget and plan your repayment. Be it paying in full or the minimum payments or in between, you can see the effect, and how much extra you are paying the bank. So, you can clear your debts faster.

About The Author

JEREMY KHO is a millennial in his early 30s. He is a self-published author, an individual investor, an engineer, and an online marketer. He had 5 years of experience in the consultancy firm in Singapore, and that experiences he acquired had helped him to think more logically and systematically in investing.

He had started his financial journey and investing in his early 20s, where he had been applying the same strategy in this Book. It is noteworthy that the strategy isn't some new idea – it's been advocated by many economists and investors, including Warren Buffett.

He had learned the idea on finances and investing during his career path, and he had learned from the books and courses on money matters, that with the correct money mindset, along with the knowledge and tool, toward financial freedom and a rich life is entirely possible.

Additional details about Jeremy, and the materials he offers can be found at:

Website : Stress Proof Your Money

Facebook : www.facebook.com/stressproofyourmoney

Twitter : twitter.com/SProofYourMoney

OTHER BOOKS BY JEREMY KHO

The Passive Aggressive Earner
(https://www.amazon.com/dp/B07B6QRNBX)

The Journey From Poor Procrastinator to Invested Millennial
(https://www.amazon.com/dp/B078PNS4TT)

The Millennial Roadmap to a Rich Life
(https://www.amazon.com/dp/B01LX2PMXD)

The Millennial Guide to Success in Stock Investing
(https://www.amazon.com/dp/B01N3XMG51)

The Millennial Guide to Success in Mutual Fund Investing
(https://www.amazon.com/dp/B01NBP1XG4)

Time Value of Money Decoded
(https://www.amazon.com/dp/B06XSNHHZL)

Being Rich? How Serious Are You?
(https://www.amazon.com/dp/B073PCQFHV/)

Thank You For Reading My Book

May I ask you a favor? If you got anything out of this book or if you have any comments. I appreciate all of your feedback and I love hearing what you have to say on the book.

Please leave me a helpful review on Amazon letting me know your thought. Your input will help make the next version of this book and my future books better.

Leave a review on this book's product page. (https://www.amazon.com/review/create-review?asin=B06XSNHHZL)

Thank You!
~Jeremy Kho~

Printed in Great Britain
by Amazon